GREATER
GREATER

PIA F. BROWER

Long Island, New York
Copyright © 2019 by Pia Florene Brower

All rights reserved. No parts of this book be reproduced by any mechanical, photographic, or electronic process, or in the form of phonographic recording; nor may it be stored in a retrieval system, transmitted, or otherwise be copied for public or private use – other than for "fair use" as brief quotations embodied in articles and reviews – without prior written permission of the publisher.

The author of this book does not dispense spiritual advice or prescribe any technique as a form of treatment for physical, emotional, or medical problems either directly or indirectly. The author intends to offer information of a general nature to help you in your quest for spiritual well-being. In the event you use any of the information in this book for yourself, which is your constitutional right, the author or publisher assume no responsibility for your actions.

Cover Design – Okomota
Editing and Layout – The Self-Publishing Maven
Interior Design – Istvan Szabo, Ifj., Sapphire Guardian International
ISBN 13: 978-1-7343951-0-5
Printed in the United States of America

ACKNOWLEDGEMENTS

Thank you Shepherd Pastor John W. Rivers, for helping me grow and constantly reminding me that God has a plan for my life. I am grateful for your teachings and our relationship.

My husband Dion: God gave me exactly what I prayed for in a husband. You are gentle yet strong, and meek. I truly thank God for you! You are an amazing husband and an amazing father to our children, Darice and Isaac. Thank you for supporting, praying and having patience. Thank you for loving me for who I am, and the person God called me to be. I am blessed! I love you Husband!

My children, Darice and Isaac. Mommy loves you so much! Always remember to keep God first in everything you do. Reach for the stars, the sky is the limit. Eyes haven't seen nor ear heard the thing that God has planned for you!

To my Mommy Rebecca Rivers, thank you for always having my back and being there for me. I appreciate you for your love, support, wisdom and for being an awesome grandmother. I love you tremendously!

To my Daddy Gerald Brown, thank you for loving me no matter what! I love you so much!

Thank you my bonus parents Wanda James and Ernest Fuller. I love you!

Thanks to my aunts and uncles, my siblings (Nicole, Eugene (SIP) Ernisha, and Elijah), cousins, nieces and nephews, which there are too many too name. However, I'm grateful that every time I needed you, you've been there. I love you!

My mentor Dr. Tonya Williams, thank you for nurturing, praying, and investing time with me. You've taught me to love me unconditionally, how to pray without ceasing and most of all to love God. I love you and am forever grateful!

My Pastor, Shepherd and Lady Tamiko Rivers: I love you!

My family, friends, faithful prayer partners and my Fab 10 sisters: You are all special to me and I'm excited to see what God has planned for you. I speak blessings over your life in the name of Jesus! I love every one of you!

My brothers and sisters in Christ: Keep standing on God's promises! Stay in the word of God and never stop believing! I love you!

My Worship Christian Center family: God placed me in this ministry for a reason and I'm so grateful that He did! I love you like family.

A special thank you Auntie Elder Katherine Ford who believed in the vision that God gave and connected me to my destiny! I love you and are forever grateful.

Auntie Eleanor, you are a prime example of diligence and obedience and proof that hard work pays off! Thank you for cutting out the pathway to follow my heart's desires. I'm thanking God for your love and guidance down throughout the years! I love you Woman of God!

Auntie Veronica, your excellent spirit has taught me that when you live for God, he can do the impossible! And when we give God a yes, we start living our best! I thank God for you and your love and unconditional support. I love you Woman of God!

Thank you Robin Devonish, The Self-Publishing Maven for your assistance on this project. You've been a mentor to me during this journey and I am forever grateful.

DEDICATION

I thank the Lord in heaven for giving me a vision to birth! I wrote this book and will write many more in the name of the Alpha and Omega, over my life! "GODS word will accomplish what he has sent it forth, for it to do." – Isaiah 55:11

I dedicate this book to my grandmother Beatrice Louise Rivers, who went home to be with the Lord. She was always there, praying for and believing in me.

INTRODUCTION

I admit that I have a colorful past of addiction, abusing my temple, making bad choices that led to incarceration, and homelessness. However, developing a relationship with Christ has changed my life and given me the vision to write.

I had a grandmother who loved me to no end. Despite what I did and said, she prayed for me, encouraged me and never judged me in my low points. She believed that God would deliver me from myself. I thank God that she had a chance to see me turn my life over to Jesus and my gift of poetic revelation about the power of Jesus, salvation, faith and freedom. I wholeheartedly believe her prayers sparked what God is doing on my life.

It's interesting where one can find the inspiration of God. Through family, friends, conversations and life circumstances, you can find His spirit, His teachings, and His revelation.

I believe words have the power to heal. Once we make the decision to carry Jesus in our hearts, we are never the same. God desires for us to be and do more. And His word says we will do GREATER works in Him.

GREATER is my poetic journey designed to stir you up on the inside. Through these pages I aim to encourage you to believe, call on Jesus, praise, pray and surrender to God.

Again, the Lord is calling you and me higher in relationship so we can live out our purpose in Him. Love, success and victory are ours in Jesus name.

CONTENTS

A Letter to Jesus 1

My Grandmother 2

Tap into Greatness 3

Greater 4

Jesus 5

Salvation 17

Faith 29

Freedom 43

Praise 53

Encouragement 65

A LETTER TO JESUS

God, I trust you with everything that You have given me. A penny for our thoughts, no it's more like a million with You. Father you said everything I touch will prosper, You fixed my attitude and helped me to grow up. You have opened my eyes and entered life into my heart. I am beyond grateful. I am spiritually minded, the way You intended me to be. I am grateful for our relationship and Your presence in my life as a father, confidant, friend and everything that I need.

   Thank you for carrying and never dropping me. Heavenly Father please don't allow me to ever drop any of what You've given or blessed with in people, spiritually, mentally, and financially.

MY GRANDMOTHER

From when I was a little girl, my grandmother prayed for me
When I felt all alone in this world, my grandmother stayed with me
She took me to church, and introduced me to Christ
And that's the best gift, I received in my life!
I'll never forget, all the times we shared
Like our conversations, our shopping and her laughter in the air
She shared in my hurts, she shared in my pain and always reminded me, they'll be better days
In life and death, she taught me about living
Like to live, like it's your last day, and to be that much more giving
Now watch and see, the growth and expansion
And know that your wisdom, will never be taken for granted
I love you now, and I loved you then
We're overcomers in Christ, there's no way, we won't win
You fought a good fight and you won
And now your free with Jesus, your life has just begun!

TAP INTO GREATNESS

I'm a living testimony by the grace of the great one
I have a great message about the greatest that's ever come
He's come to bring salvation to anyone who receives
He wants to heal the sick for everybody that's in need
His name is Christ Jesus
It is He who sits on the right hand of God interceding for us
It is He who gave His life for our sins to be forgiven
Jesus is the reason for every season and the reason we're all living
He wants to heal your heart, for those who have been broken
No matter what it feels like, Gods word has already been spoken
Daniel was in the lion's den and Joseph sold as a slave
Those men trusted God enough and because of that they were saved
Just like God delivered those men, he wants the same for you
But both those men trusted God enough, for God to come on through
Once you tap into this greatness that's available to you
You'll see joy and peace and breakthrough after breakthrough.

GREATER

Heartaches and tribulations, burdens and tears
I've considered them all and I still have no fear
Fear of failing or fear of trying
Fear of rejection or fear of dying
I've considered them all and I still have to say
I serve a great God, and to him alone do I pray
There's no need to worry, for God is with me
I am an overcomer; I have Christ in me
He's always guiding us, even when we don't see our way
God has angels on assignment, who guards us everyday
I'm walking in a greater anointing, of the GREAT I AM
I'm walking in a greater assignment; I believe God can
We walk by faith, knowing all things are possible
To get what God has in store, we must be unstoppable
God has a greater plan, just for you
And once you acknowledge it, the old way just won't do
He will open your eyes and make them brand new
Because greater is He, who lives in me, just like He'll live in you.

A 'Greater' Nugget!
Remember, you are an overcomer through Christ Jesus and that is greater than anything else!

JESUS

THAT'S WHO GOD IS!

Precept upon precept, God built this rock
Now the enemy has been defeated, so his games must stop
Stop all that lying, I know who I am, God is in control
My life with God, keeps me away from the old
God is the one, who makes everything new
Lean not to your own understanding, God is saying something to you
He is omnipotent and His grace is sufficient for you and me
Trust and believe in your heart, He has your destiny
God is the living God, can't you see
He spoke the world into existence and parted the red sea
He is life and He is hope
He is the living GOD, not the pope
Open your Bible and read what it said
From my understanding, He is the light and the living bread.

A 'Greater' Nugget!
God is Alpha and Omega and all power His hands.

MY EVERYTHING

I have everything I need; it was given to me from my savior
One thing is for sure, I have favor
Everything has changed because Christ saved me
Everything I ever imagined, even the opportunity to speak
He's given me hope and an opportunity to pray
My everything is Christ and to show others the way
I won't let Him go because He's my everything
Every time I think about Him, I open my mouth and sing
My healing, my direction, only God will get the glory
I'm grateful for everything, God has poured inside me.

A 'Greater' Nugget!
When you get with Jesus, He's all that you will ever need!

CALL ON JESUS

There is no greater love, than from the Father up above
His love is for certain and it's as gentle as a dove
Any problems that you have, He's sure to see you through
I'm constantly asking the Holy Spirit, where would I be without you?
When you call on Him, He won't let you fall
As soon as you get to calling, He'll answer the call
Spending time with the Father, it's very relevant
He can help you; it'll be time well spent
Get in His face already, go high into the deep
You're sure to get a call back, even if you go back to sleep
He desires to him from you, go ahead and speak
He's strong and mighty, our strength when we are weak
Have a new yes in your heart towards God, each and everyday
After your yes, just do your best, to stay faithful to his way
Jesus is on the main line, tell Him what you need
Just call on him, then wait on Him, I wish you Godspeed.

A 'Greater' Nugget!
God is always talking. Spend time with Him, for He's always speaking, have a heart to hear God!

JESUS MY FRIEND

Jesus sticks close, closer than any friend
With Jesus in your heart, He will carry you to the end
The kind of friend that will die for you, without you asking
That's the kind of love that is clearly everlasting
I walk with Christ everyday
The Bible says, He hears every word we say
Take confidence in knowing, your enemy cannot prevail
You can be overconfident, because my Bible says, all is well
You have greatness in your blood, winner in your genes
You've been acknowledged by God the father, that's what that means
You're joint heirs with Christ, that's rightfully yours
And once you accept it, you can't have, no more blocked doors
With Jesus as your friend, you won't and can't be blocked
Your relationship with Jesus, it can't and won't be stopped.

A 'Greater' Nugget!
God wants you to succeed. Stay in the faith, He'll be everything you need.

IT WAS JESUS

It was Jesus who died for you and me
Because Christ died, we have our necessities
Like life more abundantly
Promises to never let us down or leave
Christ you gave life, so we give you all the glory
Now I can testify, that you came before me
I've been perfected in your power
Salvation through Christ in this hour
It was Christ who said, He won't forsake you and I
It was Christ, the risen savior who died and has been revived.

A 'Greater' Nugget!
It was Jesus, who died for you! Be willing to die to self, so His spirit can live through you.

MY TEACHER JESUS

He teaches me how to listen, and teaches me what to say
I was taught how to overcome, when I learned how to obey
He taught me how to forgive
Repentance and afterwards then you can live
He teaches all things are possible, only to them that believe
And how to call on His name and to do it with authority
He teaches us by his stripes, we are healed
Teaches how to tame the tongue and how we are sealed
Sealed with His prophecies over our life
No wonder His word is sharper than any knife
With everything He teaches us, the one I love the most
Is how He teaches us, how to be led by the Holy Ghost.

A 'Greater' Nugget!
Be teachable! Acknowledge the teacher and He'll show you His way. Give Him an opportunity, to have a relationship with all of you.

HOLY GHOST

Can't you see I've been changed?
That's the Holy Ghost that signed my name
I have the Holy Ghost; I know He got me too
He changed my direction; He tells me what to do
Can't you hear it in the way I speak?
That's not me, that's the Holy Ghost flowing from the inside of me
Is the Holy Ghost a compass? Absolutely
He's always encouraging when He speaks to me
God sent His Holy Ghost after Jesus went away
He didn't leave us comfortless; the Holy Spirit is here to stay.

A 'Greater' Nugget!
God promised to leave us comfortless, so He sent the Holy Ghost.
#victorythroughchristjesus

I AM IN CHRIST JESUS

I am in Christ and He lives in me
And that's the way it's supposed to be
I am a new creature; the old things are passed away
I am healed, set free and no more bondage flowing my way
I am sanctified and filled with the Holy Spirit
Because I'm in Christ, the sky is the limit
Because I'm in Christ, greater days are ahead of me
That's the same greater, that all will see
I am in the world but not of it
I told you I'm in Christ, and I'm grateful for it
I thank God for hope and His love, that's who He is
I receive greatness, because He is mines and I am His.

A 'Greater' Nugget!
Christ has empowered us to do greater exploits. Go ahead and give God a chance and see what He will do, in you!

ASK THE HOLY SPIRIT

Just ask the Holy Spirit what to do
God will do it, I promise you
As long as you have the faith to believe
That God is faithful; He'll do it for his glory
Ask the Holy Spirit how to pray
You'll be amazed; at all you have to say
The Holy Spirit will lead you, if you let him
You'll walk by faith, and you'll have evidence
Ask the Holy Spirit, to activate your faith
Acknowledge the Holy Spirit, and what he has said
A double minded man, is unstable in everything
So just ask the Holy Spirit, which direction to take
You must depend on the Holy Spirit and that's all I have to say
Ask the Holy Spirit about everything, that is Gods perfect way.

A 'Greater' Nugget!
Jesus sent the comforter aka THE HOLY SPIRIT

JESUS WAS HERE

The times we're in right now, is different from way back then
When Christ came down to help us, and walked among all men
He came down to teach everybody and to show us all the way
He didn't care about popularity, and what people had to say
He was humbled, not double minded with a bad attitude
That why Christ deserves all our gratitude
He knew there'd be new life, in those many multitudes
It was clear because they showed up, at His every move
Our savior Jesus Christ showed up way back when
A sacrificial lamb, He was here to die for our sins.

A 'Greater' Nugget!
Christ gave of Himself, so you would know what true love looks like. He sacrificed, so that you would have an abundant life. Thank God for being saved!

GOD GIVES

God gives and He takes away
He gives us strength from day to day
God gave us sonship
And power through the Holy Spirit
God gave us a mind like Christ
You can't substitute that, even if you tried
God gives healing because it's the children bread
God gives forgiveness and made us the head
It's in His word, everything that He has given
The best thing he gave was Christ Jesus and a better living.

A 'Greater' Nugget!
What God wants to give you and I, is greater than we can imagine.

SALVATION

THIS IS MY PRAYER

My prayer is that each one of you, will know that you are saved
This is the main reason Christ, had risen from the grave
I hope and pray that you will have wisdom
And joy in the name of our savior Jesus
The prayers of the righteous, avails much
My prayers are that you will have much
Not only will you have much, I pray for overflow
That's the only way my Father knows
For you to have more abundantly on today
That's my prayer for you all the time, not just on yesterday.

A 'Greater' Nugget!
Prayer changes people hearts and situations. It's evident that when you pray, things start to happen. Invite God into your circumstances for nothing too hard for God!

I'M A BELIEVER

Can you believe in yourself? God says He can
You must believe, according to Gods' plan
Do you believe that Jesus died for your sins?
Do you believe because He did, we now win?
Do you believe the word of God or even what it says?
Do you believe you'll have eternal life? If so, move out of Gods way!
Do you believe that God is able or does it even matter?
You must believe your former days, won't be greater than your latter
Do you believe everything you got, the Lord has given
I believe in God because it's my only way of living
I believe Jesus loves you and that He really cares
I believe He's close to you, go ahead call Him nearer
Do you believe in miracles and the promise of a new life?
You must believe, for you to receive, His vision for your life.

A 'Greater' Nugget!
God has a plan for your life. Believe it and go forth in great success.

SALVATION MEANS

When you are saved by grace, you walk in expectation
That all things work together for your good, which is confirmation
That God has a plan for your life
And all things are possible, no matter the fight
It means you're not cocky but confident
That greater is he and you have his spirit that's excellent
That means you're latter will be victorious
That means no matter the storms, God will reign glorious
It means you know that God is in control
To be saved means you can open your mouth and be bold.

A 'Greater' Nugget!
Praise God for His goodness! Embrace Confidence! Expect His Greatness! Walk in Victory!

I AM IN CHRIST

I am in Christ and Christ is in me
I follow Christ and that's the way it should be
Since I am in Christ, who makes all things new
He never leaves me or forsakes me, like people will do
Since I am in Christ, who provides all my needs
All I need is His spirit, that's precious to me
Since I am in Christ, I've surrendered to authority
Not of man or some made up spirituality
I am a living witness, that there is a CHRIST
Who else would come and give me this here new life.

A 'Greater' Nugget!
Don't be deceived; when you are in Christ, your eyes are open to see.
#IKNOWIMINCHRIST

CHRIST IS PRICELESS

Do you know what I call priceless?
To go to God and openly confess
To welcome Christ in and salvation you accept
And watch Christ in you start to manifest
And just getting to know Him for your self
That's your inheritance, greater than any wealth
Priceless is the blood that Christ shed on Calvary
That gave us hope and greater destiny
When God gave us Jesus, it was for our help
Not once did He complain, after every whelp
Life without Christ is like a spoiled rotten apple
But life with Christ is priceless, He's our perfect example.

A 'Greater' Nugget!
We all were purchased by the blood of the lamb. That's priceless.

WE ARE MEMBERS, PART OF A BODY

There are many members and one body
Alpha and Omega, has made us all somebody
We are all ministers of flaming fire
To set the captives free and go out and inspire
We all should be spiritual minded, in all things
If we're not, what kind of action does that bring?
Hopeless, doubting, fear and anxiety
We're in the world but not part of their society
If God has anointed you to prophecy in His name
That's your place in the body, don't be ashamed
In the body of Christ, God got you covered
We are all members, fitly joined together.

A 'Greater' Nugget!
We all have an assignment. Trust God and do what He has called you to do for the Kingdom.

THE CHASE

Run after God, with all you got
Endure the process, even when it seems hot
Chase after God, He won't let you down
And at the end of the race, you will have a crown
Chase after righteousness
Walk in your joy and your gladness
Chase after peace, Gods authority
The blessings poured out, that means spiritual maturity
God has given us, His spirit
Just trust Him and stay in it
And the race is won, if you endure to the end
In this race called life, Jesus is our best friend
Go after God for answers and your every need
We're a spirit in a body, so let your spirit man, take the lead.

A 'Greater' Nugget!
There's joy and peace in chasing after God.

IT'S OUR JOB

We all have a job to do, for the kingdom
#1 priority is to keep our mind on Christ, or we'll be done
From the dust we came, to the dust we return
Our job is helping people, not to go to hell and burn
One of our assignments, is to be used for Gods' glory
And another title, is tell people my life story
To be a witness of how Jesus saved me
Because I was once lost and now, I'm found and set free
I'm set free because God has forgiven me
I have victory, because greater is He, that's in me
I'll pay my dues, by speaking the gospel
And while I'm working, I won't become hostile
One of our jobs, is to pray consistently
Hallelujah, we have won the victory!
So, we have work to do, and as a matter of fact
We must remind everybody, that Jesus is coming back.

A 'Greater' Nugget!
Remember, we are not our own. We are spiritual beings, living in a body. It pleases God when we seek opportunities to tell people about Him.

STOP THROWING STONES

People in glass houses, shouldn't throw stones
Anytime the flesh start talking, just leave it alone
God is displeased, with all talks of evil
Anger, gossiping and jealousy, they are all lethal
Encouraging people, is my favorite thing to do
I walk with people, who does the same thing too
What are you doing? Are you the one, throwing stones?
Do you respect the living God, if so, then make it known
Do not entertain, what people have to say
The best thing for them, is to open your mouth and pray
Encourage their hearts, if you see that they're broken
Let them hear, Gods word that's already been spoken
Rejoice in persecution, because your help is on the throne
And rejoice and rest assured, we have Jesus, our corner stone.

A 'Greater' Nugget!
God is greater than any stone what is thrown our way.

CHRIST WILL BE BACK

Christ will return, and that is a fact
If you understand one thing, Christ is coming back
The critics may try to deny
But my Bible tells me, He will crack the sky
I'm absolutely one hundred percent sure
That Jesus is the way, that is the only door
My Bible says, Christ has risen
And with that said, our sins have been forgiven
We must stay ready, right now and always
If God said it, I believe and expecting Him any day.

A 'Greater' Nugget!
I can rest in the truth that Christ will return for me and you.

IT IS WRITTEN

The Bible let us to know, that Jesus is Gods' only begotten son
It is written that Jesus surely has won
And the Bible tells us, we're precious in Gods' sight
How nothing is impossible, and we're overcomers through Christ
The Bible tells us, to stand still and see the salvation of the Lord
And that the weapon won't prosper, though it has been formed
So, release Gods' word over your life
And be strong in the Lord and the power of His might
It also advises judge not unless you'll be judged
And don't harbor unforgiveness or even hold a grudge
No matter the situation is on today
Give God back His word and declare God this is what you say
I am a witness of what the word of God can do
It's sharper than any two-edged sword, let God manifest in you.

A 'Greater' Nugget!
We can find solace in God's word for encouragement, strength and love.

FAITH

SURRENDER

I surrender my will, my way, my demands
I surrender to all things are possible, it's Your will and your plan
My thoughts for Yours, my I can't, for I can
All my being God I place in Your hands
I surrender everything, even my heart
And as I surrender to greater, greater destiny imparts
I'll move out of Gods way
I'll keep hope and I'll wait for every word you say
The last season had me feeling dry and hopeless
My new season is greatness and staying focused
Since I surrendered, destiny is ahead
I said yes to everything except being dead
What God did for me, let Him do it for you
Gods got a plan for everyone, so surrender to purpose too.

A 'Greater' Nugget!
Surrender is knowing you are everything in Christ and nothing without Him. Remember that God has a plan for you, but you must do it His way.

LET GOD TAKE THE LEAD

Let God get the glory out of your life
He'll lead you with wisdom and the power of His might
Separate from sin and let God be in charge
You'll be so happy you did; He'll bring you very far
He'll lead by His power as you trust Him more often
Let God lead no matter who's doing the talking
His ways are perfect, His words tried and true
God is omnipresent, He's already gone ahead of you
He promised to never let you fall
Whenever you need Him, just call
Let God lead He'll make your ways prosperous
And once He's leading, then you'll have success.

A 'Greater' Nugget!
When we let God take the lead, all things will work according to His perfect plan and timing.

THAT'S WHAT I BELIEVE

I believe that these are the last days
We must have assurance, that we will be okay
The prayers of the righteous avails much
Nobody should be gossiping about such and such
No matter what it may look like, that's on the outside
We all should have Jesus Christ, living on the inside
The time that we're in, the enemy wants to devour
We are living in perilous times, but God has all power
There is no other way, but to watch and to pray
Get a relationship with God, trust and obey
The Bible says, we'll have peace that passes all our understanding
And we know it's the word of God, that will only remain standing
There is no greater relationship, than the Father and the Son
Cultivate the vision and take it and run
We are living in the last days, don't you ever forget that
Jesus will be coming back soon, I believe that's a fact.

A 'Greater' Nugget!
There are blessings stored up for the true believer in Jesus Christ.

YOU ARE

God, You are strength and You are my helper
You are a present help, You are my shelter
You are the potter, I am your clay
You are hope for tomorrow, You're always making a way
God, You are my compass, going out and coming in
Because of You, we can have an expected end
You are all powerful, Alpha and Omega
Because You created me, You are my creator
Because of who You are, Great I AM
Greatness in me was always a part of Your plan.

A 'Greater' Nugget!
God is EVERYTHING we need Him to be!

I'M WALKING

You can speak to your mountain and it has to move
As you walk with Jesus, you'll see how fast things improve
If you have faith, the size of a mustard seed
Be confident and know, God will provide all your needs
Can't nobody do me like Jesus, that's the way I talk
I'm privileged to His faithfulness, I'm sure in my walk
Even in my darkest hour, while I was being defiant
God picked me up and gave me victory over my goliath
And now I'm walking by faith and not by sight
I absolutely must say, that we walk in Gods' light.

A 'Greater' Nugget!
Opening your heart and walking with God will reveal your PURPOSE.

IN THE NAME OF JESUS

In the name of Jesus, there is power in your life
If you're connected to His power, you are the light
The righteous run in and they are safe
In the name of Jesus, deliverance has surely come
All things are possible, in this day
In the name of Jesus, is what you would say
In the name of Jesus, I have a greater altitude
I am determined, I won't walk with the multitude
In the name of Jesus, bodies are healed
You got to know by now, Jesus is the real deal
Whatever you're facing, Jesus can handle it
However it's going down, don't frown, that's it!
Because in the name of Jesus, this too shall pass
It's only what we do in the name of Jesus, that will last.

A 'Greater' Nugget!
In the name of Jesus, there is great authority and power. Go ahead and use it! Don't hesitate to call on his name. That name is above all names. #JESUS

MY FEET SHALL NOT STUMBLE

My feet shall not stumble, my feet shall not fail
God has the last word, and He does all things well
We can do all things through His power
God is our strength at every hour
My help is on the way, when I look to the hills
I believe and I am confident, God will help me still
I am confident, my feet will not be taken
My feet in quicksand, I still won't be shaken
Order my steps in your word, Lord please
And keep my feet shod with the preparation of the gospel of peace.

A 'Greater' Nugget!
"The steps of a good man are ordered by the Lord." –Psalm 37:23 Let God lead the way.

WITHHOLDING NOTHING

I like to give honor, to God, who's my everything
Glory to God, I'm not holding back from my king
As He's lifted up, He's not a natural being
And as He moves upon me, It's no natural thing
I open up my mouth and let Him use me
Every word I speak, it's God who gets the glory
He did it for me and I believe for my sister
I'm withholding nothing, I'm more than a visitor
I'm withholding nothing, if that's what you thought
I didn't hold back a praise, during every battle fought
I'm not holding back my new attitude, that's my victory
God is faithful, I won't hold back, it'll be for all to see.

A 'Greater' Nugget!
When we surrender, God can reveal the 'greater' way He has for us.

THE PROMISES OF GOD

The promises of God, are yay and amen
There's always work to do, time to expand
We know the devil is a liar
He can't handle, the Holy Ghost fire
God promises to never leave or forsake you
Take God at His word, it's the best, you can do
The promises of God are yea and amen
As you start growing, you'll see Gods' great plan
That's the way it's supposed to be
His vision, has purpose and greater authority
God is faithful, and He knows how to move
Expect His promises, over each one of you.

A 'Greater' Nugget!
Be confident in knowing, that all of Gods' promises are yay and amen.

AS I AGREE

I agree with God's purpose, He has for me
I agree that, eyes have not seen
I am determined, nothing shall stop us
As I agree, greater is He, that's inside of us
That's a new way of thinking, that's the way it should be
I agree that's the way you ought to see
You will see, once you agree
That God is bigger than you and me
I agreed with His miracle to write this book
And once I did, that's all it took
There's power in agreement, I stay connected all the time
Gods spirit will have you agreeing with being divine.

A 'Greater' Nugget!
Want to live a blessed life? Trust and agree with the word of God over your life.

GODS' VISION

It had to be Gods' vision over our life
To see us free, laying aside every struggle and strife
It had to be Him, who saw us in spite of
Everything God sees, He's stirring up
Write the vison and make it plain
He sees who He called you to be, not for any gain
But to be a blessing, everywhere you stand
And declare his righteousness, to every woman and man
Your testimony might be a hot topic
But God can see, it'll be for His profit
For God to get the glory, that's really the blessing
Your obstacles could be somebody life lesson
Gods has a vision for your life, and all involves purpose
That's why He breathed new life and removed all the curses
The struggle is over, God said it, He can't lie
I speak joy and peace and Gods' vision over your eyes.

A 'Greater' Nugget!
Gods' vision over your life will exceed everything you've ever even thought about.

GOD HAS THE FINAL SAY

God has a great plan, for all of us
The Bible says, He thinks great thoughts toward us
Start running with the vision God gave
It could be worse, you could've been sleeping in your grave
Give God the glory
Because He's the author of our story
While you walk by faith, wherever you go
Everybody will know that God had the final say so.

A 'Greater' Nugget!
The best outcome is the one that is put in God's hand.

ANSWERED PRAYER

All things work together for our good
The prayers of the righteous avails much and it should
Father forgive us for our sins, I pray
That's the power He's given us, to open our mouths to say
We constantly pray for our nation
And while we're at it, we thank God for our relation
To Christ who is married to the backslider
He supplies all our needs, He's my provider
I lift my hands and I pray, help my unbelief
God will get all the glory, He's always my relief
Our connection is not a physical one
But it's through the Holy Spirit, that we tarried for from day one
I lift my hands, I kneel, and I pray
For the characteristics of my Heavenly Father in every way
My answered prayer is to see people saved
And for all people to acknowledge Him, in all their ways
I know God hears from us, whatever we say
Give Him the highest praise, then humble yourself and pray.

A 'Greater' Nugget!
There is power in prayer! Be excited that not only does God hear you; He loves to hear from you.

FREEDOM

LIBERTY

Being a Christian means you have liberty
Having a relationship with Jesus, means you have the victory
You have victory over everything working your nerves
Greater is He that's in us, believe that's the word
We have victory over our situations
That means we should have victory, across the entire nation
Every morning we wake up, Gods mercies are new
You're fortunate on today, because you have liberty too.

A 'Greater' Nugget!
"Who the son (JESUS) sets free, is free indeed!" – John 8:36

I'M FREE

I'm free from doing it my way
I said I won't sin no more, I let Gods' spirit have its way
I'm free from my past, God has washed my sins away
I won't acknowledge the old me, because it's a new day
Free from guilt and from every shame
Free from bondage, I even have a new name
Free from fear
No, I don't have to be scared
Free from pleasing everyone
Now I'm open to receive, that part of me is done
We are free and yes free indeed
Christ made the way and that's the way it'll always be.

A 'Greater' Nugget!
Don't be afraid to be free in who God has destined for you to be. Now say it after me "I AM FREE"

I AM FREE

I have been changed, now I can see
I see what Christ, did for me
Now I can see, I feel like going on
My memory has been restored, the playback is a new song
I am free from addiction
I received Christ benediction
I received miracles, and great ideas
Just by communing with the living God, He's always there
Make no mistakes, I am free indeed
God has His hands over my life, and He's moving by His authority
I am a remnant
And the enemy better not forget it!

A 'Greater' Nugget!
What Christ has done for us, made us free indeed.

SALVATION IS FREE

The consequences of sin, is death
The devil likes to fool you, until your very last breath
But repentance consists of godly sorrow
Salvation is free, it's not something you can borrow
You can't take back three years ago
But forgiveness and deliverance, will help you grow
Christ our savior, He made us free
He has made it possible, for us to have great possibilities
Isn't that wonderful, isn't that freeing
Trust and depend on him, no matter what you're seeing
He'll never leave us or forsake us, yes, I'll say it again
The best opportunity He gives to us, is to say, yes I do repent.

A 'Greater' Nugget!
Repent each day so that you can walk in a brand-new way.

MY VIEW BUT GODS PLAN

As I look through my window, I'm staring at my view
Things are looking up now, all things are brand new
My character and everything about me
I know that I've been chosen, I'm elected, Gods' royalty
A coat of many colors, I now wear
I'm stepping out on faith; I will see greater things this year!
He's the GREAT I AM and He's a promise keeper
That's what I noticed, especially when things got steeper
As I look back over my life, I thank Him for the vision
To present my body a living sacrifice, that's my decision
I know I've been changed; I have Christ to blame
My view but Gods' plan, who I was, is not the same.

A 'Greater' Nugget!
Daily question yourself and ask, 'am I living to my fullest potential and within God's plan?' I pray, you see where you're going, through Gods eyes only!

I'M IN THE KNOW

I thought I knew everything about Christ being sent
Now I truly have discovered what that meant
Christ wanted to turn people hearts, from all their wicked ways
He wanted to show somebody, He's their only way
He took our sickness and bared all our infirmities
With every striped, it canceled out every disease
Old things are behind me, I now know what that means
That means I grabbed on, to what's inside of me
There's greatness in me, now I understand
Now I know the sacrifice, was sent by Gods' hand.

A 'Greater' Nugget!
Jesus Christ is our everything and we'll ever need to know! Jesus is the only way!

I SEE DIFFERENT

No guilt, no shame, no condemnation
In God I see a greater destination
He opened my eyes, and now I can see
Greater test equals greater testimonies
Things are looking up now, and not because some fancy car
All because God said to me, do you know who you really are?
You're a child of the most high, which keeps ringing in my head
When everything tries to act up, I believe that instead
Things are looking better, I can smile, I have freedom
It's my rightful place, to serve in Gods kingdom
I'm so glad, I can see things differently
I see God doing all things supernaturally.

A 'Greater' Nugget!
It's important to seek God so you can see how powerful you are in Him.

TIME TO SEE CLEARLY

Time to see that we are the light
Lean not to your own understanding or insight
We should be focused on who God called us to be
We have to remain faithful and that's just the reality
God has given us a platform, to preach the gospel
God said to go into the highways, we are His disciples
Not everybody has to see you
But people should see, the greater that sent you
God is waiting on you to see His plan, over our lives
Time to see clearly and focus on having Gods' sight.

A 'Greater' Nugget!
There are no blinders with God. Walk by faith and believe in what God is calling for you to be. #GREATER

GOD WANTS TO KEEP YOU

Give God a reason, to keep you another day
That's what my spiritual father, used to say
Remember as his children, He has work for us to do
Be mindful of the covenant and his Holy Spirit too
God gave us an assignment, He needs for us to keep
God is watching all the time, not only when we're asleep
Speak the word only and operate in love too
And as you grow in God, His power will grow in you
Whenever temptation comes, don't fall for that deceit
Only the word of God, will keep us, on our feet
And as you go with God, do what, He sees pleasing
Do what seems worthy and God will always have a reason.

A 'Greater' Nugget!
Know that as you follow, God will lead and keep you.

PRAISE

THANKFUL

I'm thankful God gives me strength
Strength to endure at any length
I'm thankful Lord Jesus for more than a house or a car
I'm thankful for who you are
I am thankful I have Gods' grace
I am thankful; I can still seek His face
God has been good to mankind, He washed away our sins
I'm thankful that I'm blessed going out and coming back in
I'm thankful that my latter will be greater
My hope, my joy, God my creator
I'm thankful I'm the head and not the tail
I'm thankful for his promises because God never fails
He's married to the backslider, that's why I'm thankful
We don't deserve it, but I know that God is able.

A 'Greater' Nugget!
Take every moment you can to thank God for health, strength and opening your eyes each day. AMEN

I'M GRATEFUL

Lord I'm grateful for what You have shown me
Like the wisdom on how to handle prosperity
And as for poverty, it's shown me God will provide
It taught me how to look to you and how to improvise
Lord I'm grateful for Your ear, in You I can confide
Grateful when I seek Your face, from me you never hide
Most of all I'm grateful, for what's been given to us
A savior, our peace, a friend we call Jesus
Who fulfilled His destiny, according to His father's plan?
Who showed us power, some people won't understand?
And today I want to say, how grateful I am
He went before us, to set us free, God I'm grateful for the lamb.

A 'Greater' Nugget!
As often as you can, stay in a grateful place. What are you grateful for?
#IMGRATEFUL

LORD I THANK YOU

Lord I thank you for giving me salvation
Thank You Lord for healing every nation
Lord I Thank You for who You are
Thank You for being our bright shining star
Lord I Thank You for calling out my name
And since I answered, I haven't been the same
So, I thank You for kindness, that means everything
As I celebrate with every song I sing
Victorious in spite of what I looked like all along
I Thank You for purpose, my inspirational song
A relationship with You, is what I truly thank you for
Nothing else shall separate me from Christ Jesus any more
Thank You for pouring out and pouring in
You poured out Your spirit, my father, my friend.

A 'Greater' Nugget!
Thank God daily! What are you thankful for?

JUST BECAUSE

Because of who you are, I am who You say I am
Because Your grace keeps me, I will stand
Stand for righteousness
Because greater is He, that's in us
Because of your righteousness, others will know Jesus
That's because the testimony is, if God be for us
God because of who You are, my steps are ordered
And because I surrendered, I'm your daughter
I surrendered over and I'm happy that I did
God will get the glory out of my life, that won't be hid
Because Christ Jesus died and has risen from the grave
I can lift my hands and declare; I know I've been saved.

A 'Greater' Nugget!
Because He first loved us, we owe it all to Him.

WONDER WORKING POWER

There's an old saying, closed mouths won't be fed
Just like the Bible, if it's closed, you won't be led
Be careful while reading, don't twist the words around
It's increasing your faith, by the wisdom being found
Some people can't understand Gods' word, by themselves
How can they be taught without a teacher, sharing its wealth?
If you believe in His promises, from His book
Nobody can't tell you lies, not even a crook
Wonder working power, to them that believe
Wonder working power, if you have faith to receive
Gods words have power, they also have life
Wonder working power is right in front of your eyes.

A 'Greater' Nugget!
Know that you have power with and in the Lord!

DECLARATION OF PRAISE

Hallelujah to God
I surrender my all
Hallelujah is the highest praise
It's Jesus name that I call
Hallelujah righteous one
From your grace, don't let me fall
Hallelujah Holy One
By His grace and mercy, I receive my call
Victory is mine
The battle is not mines, my redeemer lives in me
God is protecting me and that's just reality
God said He would enlarge, my territory
God sent me here, to encourage somebody
God sent me to tell somebody, He's a friend indeed
God told me to remind you, that you're a righteous seed
God is a keeper, of His promises, and they'll keep coming
Remember the devil is a liar and His words are cunning
But remember who you are, victorious through Christ
You are a victor, because Jesus Christ, has paid the price
Keep your focus on Him, every single day
Go ahead and tell somebody, I walk in victory today!

A 'Greater' Nugget!
Because Christ died, you are victorious. So, declare it and thank Christ for it.

NO MORE BONDAGE

Sometimes we're our own enemy; it's not always the devil
We give up hope and never reach higher levels
We're not staying focused and putting up a fight
To have a greater destiny, we must stay in the light
No more bondage, only greater understanding
God orders our steps, so it will be a sure landing
The cares of this life, wants to keep you distracted
Nobody is perfect, but no more slacking
I believe God saved you and no, it's not an act
No more bondage anymore, and there will be no looking back.

A 'Greater' Nugget!
You are an Overcomer through Christ Jesus! Today is a new day!

HE'S MY EVERYTHING

God is my rock and my salvation
He's my strong tower, I'll witness to all generations
The last shall be first, He's my assurance of that
He's my everything; He's always got my back
He's my heavenly father; He's my best friend
My life support, in Him I win
Our heavenly father, He's a keeper of His promises
Understand God gets the glory, it'll be nothing less
God is the living God, He's the lifter of our head
God has the last say so, that's why He's my daily bread.

A 'Greater' Nugget!
God is everlasting. If you want prosperity, God got it. If you want healing, God got it.

ALL THAT I HAVE

All I have is Gods favor and His mercy
Every time I think about that, it brings joy to me
I have a praise in my lips and a dance with my feet
To top it all off, I have greater is He
I have the old things behind me
Nobody can do nothing about it, I have Gods' authority
Since practicing holiness, I have greater responsibility
I have power over all the power of the enemy
I have love, I have joy and I have peace
I have a greater determination to see my destiny.

A 'Greater' Nugget!
Having Christ as your personal savior, you'll have everything you need.

NOT THE SAME LOVE SONG

God You are worthy, and I lift my hands to praise You
My redeemer, my counselor, where would I be without You?
My way maker, my promise keeper, our light in the darkness
You are always there to help us, when we make a mess
My song simply says, great and mighty is our God
My redeemer draws near, near to my heart
As I wait on you, I look to the hill from which comes my help
Every word from Gods' mouth makes my heart melt
I have joy, I have peace, everything has changed
My lyrics shout hallelujah how I love to call His name.

A 'Greater' Nugget!
Most people march to the beat of their own drums, but dance in the expression of the Holy Spirit. You'll be glad you did.

ENCOURAGEMENT

GOD IS WAITING ON YOU

Take your mind off being depressed
God is waiting on you, to come with a yes
God is waiting on you, to repent and confess
God really wants you free from all that stress
God is great at making crooked paths straight
And as it happens, everything you'll forsake
God is waiting for you to clean up your heart
He'll impart knowledge, right from the start
God wants a yes, so there won't be any doubt
That He made you clean from the inside out
Stop waiting on people, God is waiting on you
Let him order your steps, and do the impossible through you.

A 'Greater' Nugget!
God wants you to serve him with your whole heart. You can't have one foot in and one foot out.

LEAN ON HIS PROMISES

The promises of God, are yay and amen
Stay confident, no matter the circumstance
Nothing is impossible, if God said it, you will see
See, I was once was a mess, but look how God delivered me
I'm not ashamed of the gospel or my testimony
Even then God promised He'll always be there for me
When I wanted to give up, He never let me down
I thank God for His faithfulness, He always stayed around
My testimony is evidence, if you have faith, God has the power
He is the Great I Am, our heavenly father
God kept His promises while He covered my life
He protected me and covered me, now I'm my husband's wife
You must to try His words; they are tried, and they are true
Lean on His promises and see what He has in store for you!

A 'Greater' Nugget!
Trust and believe God and watch him do it! "Let us hold fast the profession of our faith without wavering, for he is faithful that promised." – Hebrews 10:23 KJV

GET BACK UP AGAIN

God picks us up, when we have fallen
We have a new chapter, a higher calling
We are His elect, His chosen generation
We get up, and with greater determination
With Gods' authority I pass all the tests
And with each step, is the key to my happiness
At times I'm going through I ask, what would Jesus do?
It still amazes me how He kept going through
So, we must keep going, because it's part of the master's plan
Keep going in the things of God and always get back up again.

A 'Greater' Nugget!
No matter how hard you've fallen, fight to get back up. "For a just man falls seven times and gets back up again, but the wicked shall fall into mischief." – Proverbs 24:16

THE BEST IS YET TO COME

If I believe it, I'll receive it
By faith only, that's how I conceived it
I'm in my season of victory and nothing less
Success to me, is not walking around stressed
The prophecy is what He gave
And it's guaranteed to not be late
This is our season, of our success
Not the season to operate in our flesh
Your success, might be different from mines
It may be strength, money or just peace of mind
Wherever you are, decree it over your life
The best is yet to come, declare it with all your might.

A 'Greater' Nugget!
Greater days are ahead despite where you are or what you're going through. Learn to trust God!

TELL THE ENEMY NO!

Refuse to be sick, refuse the more pain
Refuse to be overlooked, refuse no more gain
Tell the enemy no, to all his games
Let him know you have the victory, once Jesus came
Let's refuse to walk, in the wrong attitude
Be mindful to stay looking ahead, to a greater avenue
A greater focus, Gods word already went out
Tell the enemy no, be bold as you go about
We will not be ignorant to the enemy devices
We will tell the enemy no, every time.

A 'Greater' Nugget!
"When the enemy comes against you, God will lift a standard all around his children." – Isaiah 59:19

HOW TO RECEIVE

It's through Christ we receive, grace and mercy
That's more powerful than any degree
How do you receive?
The main key is to ask confidently
Knowing God hears everything you say
And have a believing heart when you pray
Ask me how to receive
And I'll tell you, God gives to all men liberally
Asking is how you receive
Receiving the one who supplies all our needs
Jesus Christ is the only way to receive
He is the rewarder to them that diligently seek.

A 'Greater' Nugget!
Daily praise God from whom all blessings flow!

YOU ARE HOPE FOR TOMORROW

You're not in your tomorrow, you don't know who you are
You have greatness inside of you, you must go very far
God has His hands on you, if not, you'd probably be dead
But your life without Jesus, is like the walking dead
God can take your mess and give you a new season
God can bless you for greatness and in a new season
Your testimonies, will help someone see
See the God in you and greater possibilities
God can take your brokenness and use it for His glory
He can take your unforgiveness and make a great love story
If God can use me, He can use anything, including you
You have so much hope for tomorrow, that's a sure promise to you.

A 'Greater' Nugget!
God is real and His possibilities are endless! Put your hope in what He says. Greater is at the door!

ALL THE BEST

All the best for you, is what God really wants
You have a new day, is that what you really want?
Greater opportunities mean greater opposition
But God has all power, stand still in your position
The devil is a liar, that keeps playing in my head
Let God have the glory, you'll have victory instead
All He wants from us, is to turn from our evil ways
God wants people, that will humble themselves and pray
God really wants, a blessing for your house
He's very powerful, He deserves a praise, from our mouth
Greater storms mean greater testimonies
God gave us His best, which is Christ, the King of glory!

A 'Greater' Nugget!
God gave His best; we should give Him the same.

THE TIME IS COME

I speak victory over your life, you are anointed
God has stepped in and you've been appointed
Your breakthrough is here, God said you're coming out
God is magnificent, and He already said it, don't doubt
The adversary thought he had you, but God stepped in
You are already chosen, that means you win
Your path is looking clear, exercise your faith
You've gained knowledge, now walk in His perfect way
The time is come, for a relationship with Jesus Christ
He already signed me up, now come see what it's like.

A 'Greater' Nugget!
The time is here for us to confess or re-dedicate our lives to Christ; the best decision.

COME OUT THE WILDERNESS

Leave behind, wilderness mentality
Which means, make God your top priority
God wants to see us grow
God is truly with us, He watches, as we go
Stop walking in circles, our deliverer, draws nigh
Stop lying to yourself, time to make up your mind
Start to grow in godly character, and watch what you say
Every time you go to lead, just move out the way
That's wilderness mentality, time to grow up
Time to seek the face of God, that's how you show up
Your destiny awaits you, time to stop stalling
Come out the wilderness for good, why? Because your destiny is calling.

A 'Greater' Nugget!
Gentle reminder, a seven-day journey turned into forty years for the children of Israel. Don't stay where you are, keep growing in God.

CONSIDER IT DONE

Acknowledge God, in all your ways
And as you trust Him, He'll guide your way
Consider it done, when you ask in prayer
Keep walking by faith and constantly, He'll be near
Ask without wavering, knowing He is faithful and just
Gods' a keeper of His word, just wait and trust
Consider it done, when you seek, you'll find Him
Consider it done, in times of trouble, to get out of sin
God hears your prayers, start interceding, on behalf of others
God will make a way of escape, while you're praying, for your brother
The weapon may form, but it will not prosper
That's the kind of relationship, I have with my father.

A 'Greater' Nugget!
If God said it, we can consider it done! God is more than faithful!

DECLARATION TO DECLARE

Now say it with me:
I have everything I need, according to grace and mercy
I believe everything the Lord says about me
I am more than a conqueror, in the name of Jesus
I have the victory, through Christ my savior
I am a child of the most high power
I am an overcomer, because Christ lives in me
I receive my miracles, for the Bible says, miracles, signs and wonders shall follow me
I can do all things through Christ, who strengthens me
And no weapon formed against me shall prosper, in Jesus name
I've been given power, over all the power of my enemy
I am assured that God will use me and do it for His glory
I am a righteous seed of the most high God
I believe God will do great things in my life
I am forgiven
I have angels all around me
I'm assured that it all works for my good
God is a keeper of His word
God is preparing me, for greater
Nothing is impossible
Let the weak, say that your strong
Because you're in Christ, that's your new song.

Nothing is impossible, at least that's what God showed me
Nothing is impossible with Him, He has power and authority
Nothing is impossible, if it's in God's word, ask and receive
No weapon formed against me, is my greatest testimony
Stand on His word and believe, that God is able
He is the living God and He's never once unstable
In the name of the father, son and the Holy Ghost
Nothing is impossible, I believe, the Lord of hosts
I have greater testimonies, that God has given to me
All things are possible, if you trust in God and only believe.

A 'Greater' Nugget!
God is Alpha and Omega. There is nothing too hard for him.

THROUGH THE FIRE

I've been through the fire and I didn't get burned
God uses everything, to be a lesson learned
God uses people and certain situations
All for His purpose and our elevation
I've been through the fire, but I didn't get burned
That is behind me and I'll take what I have learned
I'll take it as I come in and as I go out
I take everything and declare I'm sold out
To God and His purpose and His plans over my life
Yes, I have a lot of testimonies, but it came with a great price
For great is our God, that has given me a new day
The fire didn't kill me, so I'm grateful, in every way
Yea though I walk, through the valley, of the shadow of death
God has shown me greater, through every storm and every test
Thank God, I don't look like what I've been through
God is keeping me, rest assured, He's keeping, every one of you.

A 'Greater' Nugget!
Just believe! God has His hands over all of us.

POWER TRIPPING

I'm power tripping over Gods glory
I'm power tripping, that God saved a sinner like me
See I was incarcerated, by grace I've been saved
My mind was made up, no more heading to the grave
I'm power tripping over, I'm my husband's wife
And how God opened, my womb and gave me new life
I stay power tripping, over grace and mercy
And how God protected me, even from me
There's power in victory, power in praise
There's power to believe, that Jesus really saves
I stay power tripping, that God has all power, in His hands
And has dominion and majesty, over the entire land.

A 'Greater' Nugget!
Nobody can deny the power of the living God! If you're going to power trip, let it be over God and all He has done.

THE GREATEST LOVE STORY

I celebrate the greatest love story
How God made us kingdom minded, all for His glory
We have work to do, to show forth His love
God separated us, being gentle as a dove
Christ went to the cross, as a sacrificial lamb
Now He has a testimony, greater than any man
As He was hanging, up there on the cross
He said father, "forgive their trespasses," that's love
He laid down His life, just so you can live
The least you can do, is learn how to forgive
He first loved us, so now we love Him
The greatest love story is how we became Christians.

A 'Greater' Nugget!
Learn to love others as Christ loved us.

GOD IS RETURNING IT BACK

All that the enemy stole, God is giving back double
The enemy already knows that he's in trouble
I'm getting back double respect, my body is healed
Just to name a few that the enemy tried to steal
God said beauty for our ashes
And that He'll turn our mourning into dancing
God is always up to something, I'm not playing
Joy and peace are the prophecy that I'm saying
It's the big pay back, double for your shame
Expect God to give you back your name
God is returning everything, except for His word
Get excited, all God has for you is about to return.

A 'Greater' Nugget!
"God has spoken once; Twice I have heard this: That power *belongs* to God."
– Psalm 62:11

STOP LOOKING BACK

Our past was very dark, I believe our future is bright
If you excepted Christ as your savior, you now have life
Everything that tripped you up, it's passed away
There is greater ahead, we will not look back, no way
He bought us too far, to leave me or you
Old things are behind us, our mind is staying renewed
Stop with the old way of thinking
That's a solid way, that you'll begin sinking
The struggle is all over, that is great news
Don't look back now, get what God has in store for you.

A 'Greater' Nugget!
Don't look back! Let 'it' go and give it to the one, who has all power in His hands, able to heal and makes all things new.

WALK INTO HIS PROMISE

God is challenging you, to walk by faith
In total confidence, doing it His way
In victory, for the battle is not ours
Walk in authority, because He has given you power
Walk and acknowledge Him, every hour
Walk in greatness, declaring victory in what you say
As you're walking with Jesus, trust and obey
Walk in the word, talk to God and walk in your new day
Walk in His promises, you'll always have confirmation
And as you walk, He'll constantly give you revelation
That He's always guiding your every footstep
Stay walking until you breathe your very last breath.

A 'Greater' Nugget!
Walk in what God has for you! Recite this now… "For the Lord is my confidence and keeps our foot from being taken." – Proverbs 3:26

YOU GOT POWER

You have power over the enemy
Use it in Jesus name, trust me
You have wonder working power in the name of Jesus
Now declare in the atmosphere, nothing can harm us
God gave us dominion over everything in the earth
Dominion and authority, now why are you so hurt?
Death and life are in the power of the tongue
Even your tongue has power, go get the devil on the run
God gave us power to lay hands on the sick
If you have a situation, speak life over it
Be confident knowing, that you have power in the name of Jesus
And His power is working down from the inside of us.

A 'Greater' Nugget!
There's power in the name of JESUS! Stay connected to Him, that's your resource.

TOMORROW

Don't worry about tomorrow, there'll be time for that
Celebrate this day, the Lord has made, let that be that
God has gone before us, and straightened crooked paths
God is in control, there's no reason to be sad
God wants you to have hope in your tomorrow
Be concerned for what? You shall lend and not borrow
Tomorrow is not promised, so use wisdom in your today
No matter what it looks like, victory is on the way
He'll make our ways prosperous and He will get the glory
I don't worry how it'll get done, God always ahead of me.

A 'Greater' Nugget!
"So, I tell you to stop worrying about what you will eat, drink, or wear. Isn't life more than food and the body more than clothes." – Matthew 6:25 (God's word translation)

SIMPLY THE BEST

What God has for you, is simply His best
What that means for you, is great success
He has given you, everything you asked for
But more than you can ask for, is what He has in store
Don't forget to ask for favor
And while you're at it, ask Him to help, your neighbor
He's a God who can't leave
I'm look forward to seeing what's up His sleeve
He's a God, you can depend on, yes you can
Simply the best, He has for you, stop depending on man.

A 'Greater' Nugget!
Simply the best is what God gave us, when he gave Christ. If you believe that, then you already received the best.

www.ingramcontent.com/pod-product-compliance
Lightning Source LLC
Chambersburg PA
CBHW081233080526
44587CB00022B/3933